Sing Hey
for
Christmas Day!

poems selected by
Lee Bennett Hopkins

illustrations by
Laura Jean Allen

Sing hey! Sing hey!
For Christmas Day;
Twine mistletoe and holly,
For friendship glows
In winter snows,
And so let's all be jolly!

Anon.

Harcourt Brace Jovanovich
New York and London

also edited by Lee Bennett Hopkins
HEY-HOW FOR HALLOWEEN!
GOOD MORNING TO YOU, VALENTINE

Every effort has been made to trace the ownership of all copyrighted material and
to secure the necessary permissions to reprint these selections. In the event of any
question arising as to the use of any material, the editor and the publisher, while
expressing regret for any inadvertent error, will be happy to make the necessary
correction in future printings. Thanks are due to the following for permission to
reprint the copyrighted material listed below:

THE BOBBS-MERRILL COMPANY, INC., for "Christmas Time" by Lee Bennett
Hopkins from *Charlie's World*, text copyright © 1972 by Lee Bennett Hopkins,
illustrations © 1972 by Charles Robinson.

THOMAS Y. CROWELL COMPANY, INC., for "Country Christmas" by Aileen
Fisher from *Skip Around the Year* by Aileen Fisher, Copyright © 1967 by Aileen
Fisher; and for "Merry Christmas" by Aileen Fisher from *Feathered Ones and
Furry* by Aileen Fisher, Copyright © 1971 by Aileen Fisher.

E. P. DUTTON & CO., INC., for "Day Before Christmas" by Marchette Chute
from *Rhymes About the City* by Marchette Chute. Copyright, 1946, renewal ©
1974 by Marchette Chute.

AILEEN FISHER for "December" from *That's Why*, published by Thomas Nel-
son & Sons, 1946.

HARCOURT BRACE JOVANOVICH, INC., for *"little tree"* by E. E. Cummings.
Reprinted from his volume, *Complete Poems 1913-1962*. Copyright, 1925, 1953,
by E. E. Cummings.

HARPER & ROW, PUBLISHERS, INC., for "Otto" by Gwendolyn Brooks from
Bronzeville Boys and Girls by Gwendolyn Brooks. Copyright © 1956 by Gwendolyn Brooks Blakely; and for "Counting the Days" by James S. Tippett from

Crickety Cricket! The Best-Loved Poems of James S. Tippett. Text copyright © 1973 by Martha K. Tippett.

MARGARET HILLERT for "Christmas Lullaby" from *Farther Than Far*, Copyright © 1969 by Margaret Hillert.

HOUGHTON MIFFLIN COMPANY for "Christmas Eve Rhyme" by Carson McCullers from *Sweet as a Pickle, Clean as a Pig* by Carson McCullers. Copyright © 1964 by Carson McCullers and Rolf Gerard.

MAY JUSTUS for "Signs of Christmas" from *Winds A-Blowing*, Copyright © 1971 by Abingdon Press.

MACMILLAN PUBLISHING CO., INC., for "What can I give Him" from *Sing-Song* by Christina Rossetti.

MC INTOSH AND OTIS, INC., for "Presents" by Myra Cohn Livingston from *A Crazy Flight and Other Poems* by Myra Cohn Livingston. Copyright © 1969 by Myra Cohn Livingston.

HAROLD OBER ASSOCIATES INCORPORATED for "Carol of the Brown King" by Langston Hughes. Copyright © 1958 by Crisis Publishing Co.

A. BARBARA PILON for "Fir Tree Tall" by Joan Hanson from *Concrete Is Not Always Hard*, edited by A. Barbara Pilon, copyright © 1972 by A. Barbara Pilon.

CHARLES SCRIBNER'S SONS for "Christmas Eve" by Marion Edey from *Open the Door* by Marion Edey and Dorothy Grider. Copyright 1949 Marion Edey and Dorothy Grider.

WESTERN PUBLISHING COMPANY, INC., for "Stay, Christmas" by Ivy O. Eastwick from *Story Parade*, copyright 1952 by Story Parade, Inc.

YALE UNIVERSITY PRESS for "Bundles" by John Farrar from *Songs for Parents*, 1921.

Library of Congress Cataloging in Publication Data
Main entry under title:

Sing hey for Christmas Day!

SUMMARY: An anthology of poetry reflecting
various aspects of the Christmas season.
1. Christmas—Juvenile poetry.   2. Children's
poetry. [1. Christmas poetry] I. Hopkins, Lee
Bennett.   II. Allen, Laura Jean.
PZ8.3.S615   821'.008'033   75-6612
ISBN 0-15-274960-8

To Charles J. Egita
with a merry and a happy
and a hey!

DECEMBER

I like days
with a snow-white collar,
and nights when the moon
is a silver dollar,
and hills are filled
with eiderdown stuffing
and your breath makes smoke
like an engine puffing.

I like days
when feathers are snowing,
and all the eaves
have petticoats showing,
and the air is cold
and the wires are humming,
but you feel all warm . . .
with Christmas coming.

Aileen Fisher

CHRISTMAS IS COMING

Christmas is coming, the geese are
    getting fat,
Please to put a penny in an old
    man's hat;
If you haven't got a penny, a
    ha'penny will do.
If you haven't got a ha'penny, God
    bless you.

Anonymous

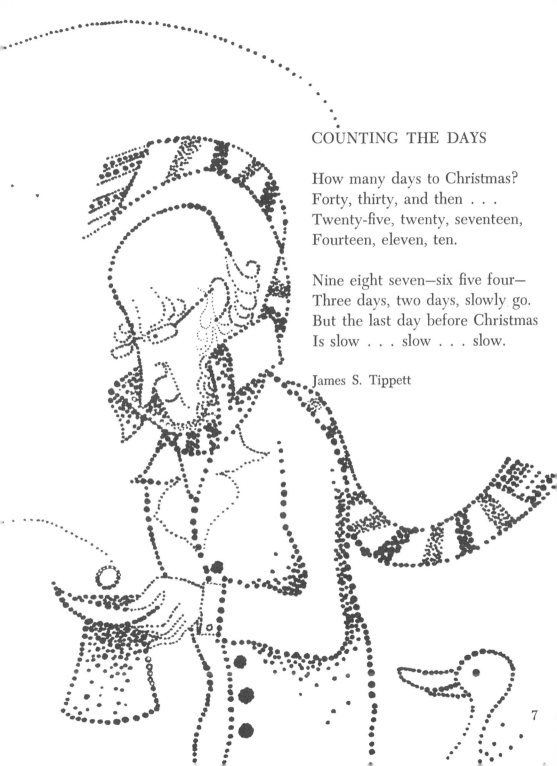

COUNTING THE DAYS

How many days to Christmas?
Forty, thirty, and then . . .
Twenty-five, twenty, seventeen,
Fourteen, eleven, ten.

Nine eight seven—six five four—
Three days, two days, slowly go.
But the last day before Christmas
Is slow . . . slow . . . slow.

James S. Tippett

7

SIGNS OF CHRISTMAS

Dancing, prancing
Here and there,
Round a corner,
Up a stair,
Through a doorway,
Down a street—
Hurry, scurry,
Go the feet.
Hustling, bustling
In and out,
Folks so gaily
All about.
From the signs
We see and hear,
Christmas time
Is very near!

May Justus

CHRISTMAS TIME

I love the tinsel
I love the bells
I love the presents Santa Claus sells.

I love the red
I love the green
I love the Christmas trees I've seen.

But—

I hate the winter
I hate the sleet
I hate my cold and stinging feet.

I hate the wind and ice and grime
Why can't Christmas come
In summertime?

Lee Bennett Hopkins

BUNDLES

A bundle is a funny thing,
It always sets me wondering;
For whether it is thin or wide
You never know just what's inside.

Especially on Christmas week,
Temptation is so great to peek!
Now wouldn't it be much more fun
If shoppers carried things undone?

John Farrar

DAY BEFORE CHRISTMAS

We have been helping with the cake
    And licking out the pan,
And wrapping up our packages
    As neatly as we can.
And we have hung our stockings up
    Beside the open grate,
And now there's nothing more to do
    Except
           To
              Wait!

Marchette Chute

PRESENTS

I have counted every present with my name.
There are four.
>One rattles like a game.
>One's a book. (I can read the title
>   through the paper.)
>I shook one, but it didn't make a sound.
>One's too round to be what I wanted.

>Maybe there are more than four.
>(I believe there must be others
>Hidden, waiting, for
>Christmas Eve.)

Myra Cohn Livingston

little tree
little silent Christmas tree
you are so little
you are more like a flower

who found you in the green forest
and were you very sorry to come away?
see   i will comfort you
because you smell so sweetly

i will kiss your cool bark
and hug you safe and tight
just as your mother would,
only don't be afraid

look   the spangles
that sleep all the year in a dark box

dreaming of being taken out and allowed to shine,
the balls the chains red and gold the fluffy threads,

put up your little arms
and i'll give them all to you to hold
every finger shall have its ring
and there won't be a single place dark or unhappy

that when you're quite dressed
you'll stand in the window for everyone to see
and how they'll stare!
oh but you'll be very proud

and my little sister and i will take hands
and looking up at our beautiful tree
we'll dance and sing
"Noel Noel"

e. e. cummings

FIR TREE TALL

Fir
tree tall
Lights glittering
Bright tinsel hung
Shimmering, glimmering
Laughter shining in the eyes
of boys
and girls
Lovely lovely
Christmas tree.

Joan Hanson

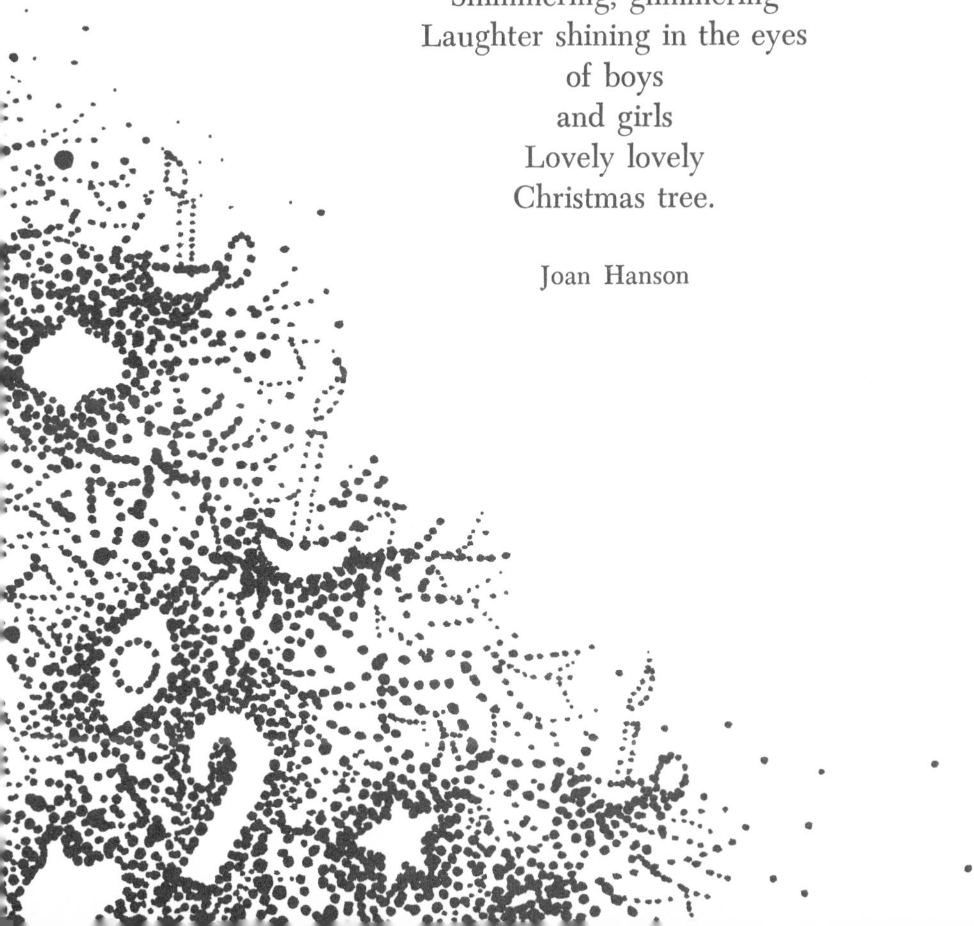

CHRISTMAS EVE RHYME

My best friend is Jimmy
He has no chimney.
So what will happen at Christmas time?
When Santa flies over the houses
And stops at each chimney
Will he skip Jimmy
Who has no chimney?

Carson McCullers

CHRISTMAS EVE

On a winter night
When the moon is low
The rabbits hop on the frozen snow.
The woodpecker sleeps in his hole in the tree
And fast asleep is the chickadee.

Twelve o'clock
And the world is still
As the Christmas star comes over the hill.
The angels sing, and sing again:
"Peace on earth, goodwill to men."

Marion Edey

from

GO TELL IT ON THE MOUNTAIN

Go tell it on the mountain,
Over the hills and everywhere,
Go tell it on the mountain,
That Jesus Christ is born.

Anonymous

CAROL OF THE BROWN KING

Of the three Wise Men
Who came to the King,
One was a brown man,
So they sing.

Of the three Wise Men
Who followed the Star,
One was a brown king
From afar.

They brought fine gifts
Of spices and gold
In jeweled boxes
Of beauty untold.

Unto His humble
Manger they came
And bowed their heads
In Jesus' name.

Three Wise Men,
One dark like me—
Part of His
Nativity.

Langston Hughes

23

What can I give Him
  Poor as I am?
If I were a shepherd
  I would bring a lamb,
If I were a Wise Man
  I would do my part,—
Yet what I can I give Him,
  Give my heart.

Christina Rossetti

LONG, LONG AGO

Winds through the olive trees
    Softly did blow,
Round little Bethlehem
    Long, long ago.

Sheep on the hillside lay
    Whiter than snow;
Shepherds were watching them,
    Long, long ago.

Then from the happy sky,
    Angels bent low,
Singing their songs of joy,
    Long, long ago.

For in a manger bed,
    Cradled we know,
Christ came to Bethlehem,
    Long, long ago.

Anonymous

OTTO

It's Christmas Day. I did not get
The presents that I hoped for. Yet,
It is not nice to frown or fret.

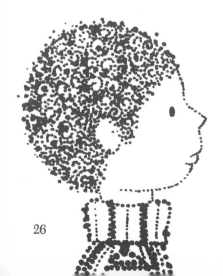

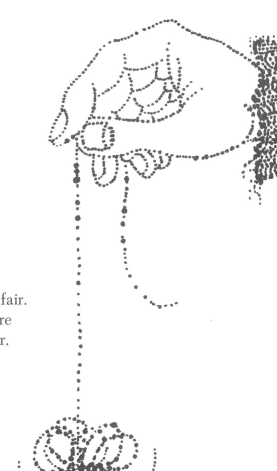

To frown or fret would not be fair.
My Dad must never know I care
It's hard enough for him to bear.

Gwendolyn Brooks

COUNTRY CHRISTMAS

Let's hang up some suet
for juncos and jays,
let's put out some hay for the deer,
let's throw in some corn
where the cottontail stays,
this holiday season of year.

Let's scatter some millet
and barley and wheat—
it isn't much trouble or fuss
to give all the wild folk
a holiday treat
so they can have Christmas, like us!

Aileen Fisher

MERRY CHRISTMAS

I saw on the snow
when I tried my skis
the track of a mouse
beside some trees.

Before he tunneled
to reach his house
he wrote "Merry Christmas"
in white, in mouse.

Aileen Fisher

STAY, CHRISTMAS

Stay, Christmas!
Stay, Christmas!
Do not go
Away, Christmas.
Laughter jolly,
Lanterns, holly,
Bells ringing,
Children singing,
All things glad
Nothing sad . . .
Oh, Stay, Christmas!
Stay, Christmas.
Do not go
Away, Christmas.

Ivy O. Eastwick

A CHRISTMAS LULLABY

Hushaby, rockaby, softly to sleep,
Soft as the snow that is drifting and blowing.
Hushaby, rockaby, shadows are deep
Blue on the snow that is endlessly snowing.
Sleep like the animals sleepily curled
In soft little nests in a winter white world.
Hushaby, rockaby, till the stars creep
Into a day that is shining and glowing.

Margaret Hillert

INDEX